BORED

by Meg Gaertner

The Child's World
childsworld.com

Published by The Child's World®
1980 Lookout Drive • Mankato, MN 56003-1705
800-599-READ • www.childsworld.com

Photographs ©: Shutterstock Images, cover (face and hand), cover (eyes), 1 (face and hand), 1 (eyes), 5, 6, 17, 19; Jingjits Photography/ Shutterstock Images, 9; Maria Symchych/ Shutterstock Images, 10; LightField Studios/ Shutterstock Images, 13; India Picture/ Shutterstock Images, 14; iStockphoto, 20, 22 (top left), 22 (top right); Hugh Stonelan/ iStockphoto, 22 (bottom left); Valua Vitaly/ iStockphoto, 22 (bottom right)

Design Elements: Shutterstock Images

ISBN Hardcover: 9781503828049
ISBN Paperback: 9781622434640
LCCN: 2018944226

Printed in the United States of America
PA02395

ABOUT THE AUTHOR

Meg Gaertner is a children's book author and editor who lives in Minnesota. When not writing, she enjoys dancing and spending time outdoors.

CONTENTS

Chapter One

LIAM'S WEEKEND

Liam woke up Saturday morning. It was raining. He could not go outside to play. He wanted something to do.

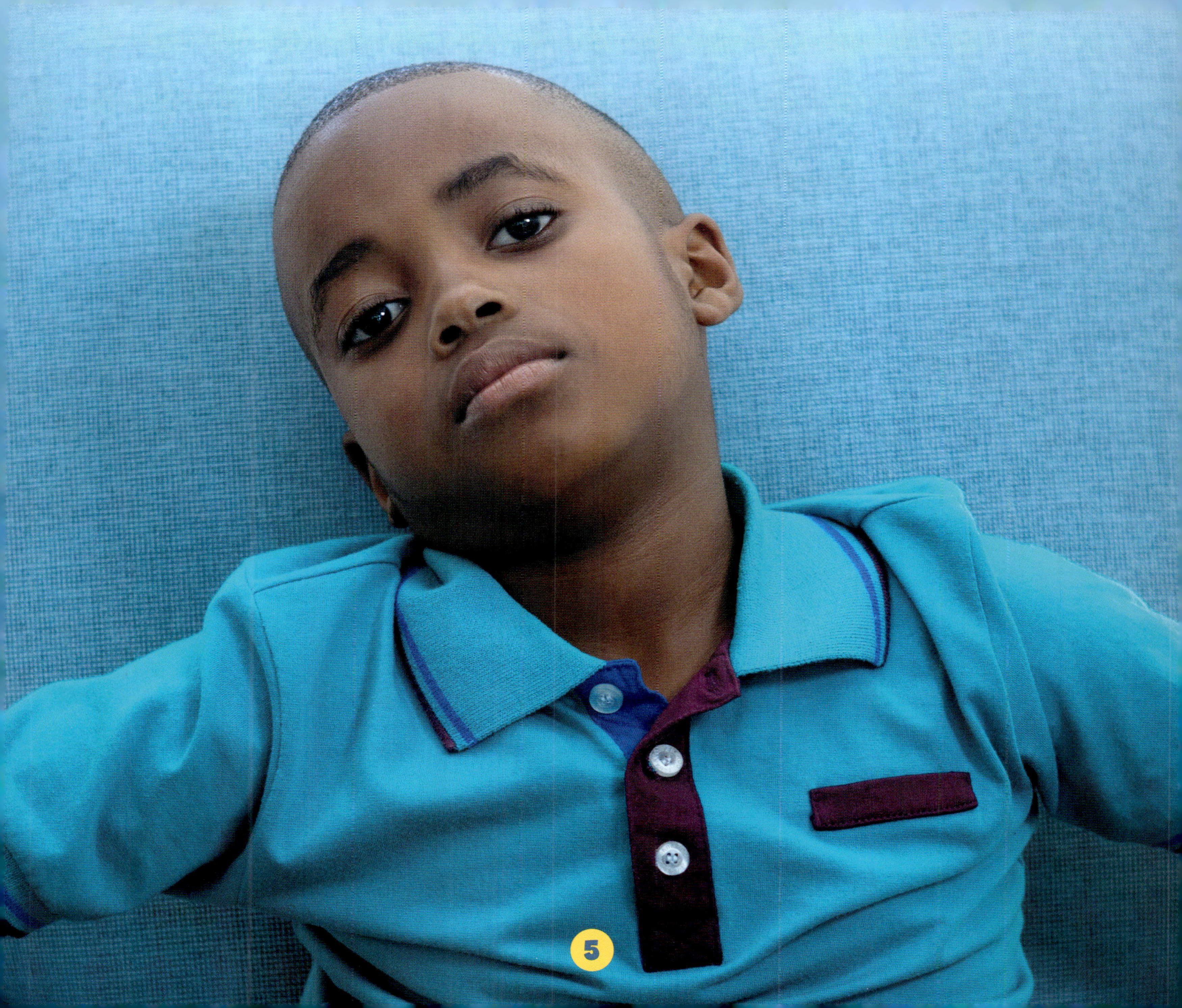

His mom was at work. His sister had homework. His dad was busy with chores. Liam was bored. He felt there was nothing to do.

Chapter Two

BEING BORED

Sometimes people have a lot of energy. They want to do something. But nothing seems interesting enough. They feel bored.

You might get **distracted** easily. You may even feel as if there is nothing to do. Everyone feels bored sometimes.

It can help to find something to **focus** on. You can be creative. Make up a game. Write a story. Paint a picture.

It can also help to tell others how you feel. They might have ideas for things you could do.

It is okay to be bored. The feeling will not last forever. You will find something to be interested in.

THINK ABOUT IT

Can you think of a time when you were bored?

Chapter Three

HELPING OTHERS

You can help others who are bored. You can create a fun game. You can **suggest** different activities.

People who are bored might seem distracted or uninterested. That is okay. You can still include them. You can still be their friend.

WHO IS BORED?

Can you tell who is bored? Turn to page 24 for the answer.

A

B

C

D

GLOSSARY

distracted (diss-TRAKT-ed) To be distracted is to be unable to focus. When you are distracted, your mind jumps from idea to idea.

focus (FOH-kuss) To focus is to think about something or someone. When you focus on something, you give your mind something to do.

suggest (sug-JEST) To suggest something is to put it forward as an idea. A friend may suggest different activities to help when you feel bored.

TO LEARN MORE

Books

Gaertner, Meg. ***Disappointed***. Mankato, MN: The Child's World, 2019.

Kreul, Holde. ***My Feelings and Me***. New York, NY: Skyhorse Publishing, 2018.

Moore-Mallinos, Jennifer. ***A Whole Bunch of Feelings***. Hauppauge, NY: Barron's Educational Series, 2018.

Web Sites

Visit our Web site for links about being bored:
childsworld.com/links

Note to Parents, Teachers, and Librarians: We routinely verify our Web links to make sure they are safe and active sites. So encourage your readers to check them out!

INDEX

Page 22 answer: **A**